Siddharth Govindarajan

100 Percent Happiness Guaranteed in 99 Pages

16 secrets that have consistently contributed to my happiness

AUTHOR: SIDDHARTH GOVINDARAJAN

Siddharth Govindarajan

About the Author

Siddharth Govindarajan is a FIDE-rated chess player, blog writer, and passionate violin enthusiast. He holds a master's degree in BUSINESS ANALYTICS from the University of Texas at Dallas, USA and thrives on uncovering insights through data analysis.

His journey has taken him across countries and cultures, engaging with people from all walks of life. Along the way, he observed a surprising pattern—despite wealth, success, or status, true happiness often remained elusive. This realization sparked a personal mission: to help others rediscover joy in simple truths.

Driven by a deep desire to make a meaningful impact, Siddharth distilled his insights into this concise and accessible guide. His goal? To bring clarity, comfort, and a spark of happiness to every reader—without complexity, without high costs, and in just 99 pages.

Preface

Dear reader,

Congratulations on making it to this world. Did you know that, during a human lifespan, a female body produces approximately anywhere between 300,000 and 500,000 eggs, while a male produces approximately anywhere between 40,000,000 and 1,800,000,000 sperm cells.

1,800,000,000 sperm possibilities x 500,000 egg possibilities = **900,000,000,000,000** which is **900 trillion**. Amongst the 900 trillion possibilities, it was you who survived and became a human being. [P1] [P2]

Each one of us are unique, much like a snowflake [P3] that does not resemble another. Even, identical twins have different fingerprints [P4], highlighting the distinctiveness and specialness of each person. Today and now is the time you will start realizing that you are special.

The purpose of this book is to help readers dig up your lost happiness or keep it shining bright if you've already found it. Although I may not know you personally, I believe that you deserve happiness.

It is important to recognize that happiness contributes significantly to life satisfaction, rather than solely focusing on the accumulation of wealth. Am I trying to say that money is not important, and money won't buy you happiness? Definitely not. Sure, money can buy you fancy stuff, but it won't buy you a permanent smile on your face. While it is important to save money, merely accumulating wealth will not sustain long-term happiness. It is advisable to seek activities and pursuits that provide satisfaction and fulfillment.

Charlie Chaplin, the renowned comedian and Academy Award winner, is celebrated for his enduring ability to evoke laughter through his unique use of body language and silent scripts. He once remarked, *"A Day without laughter is a day wasted"*. [P5] Let us incorporate this wisdom into our lives by making it a priority, goal, and intention to find moments of laughter throughout each day.

FigureP.1: Charlie Chaplin – This picture was generated by ChatGPT

In this book, I'll share some useful tips to stay happy and tackle life's challenges head-on.

Let us start with a simple question - What do you think will make a happy person sad and a sad person happy? The best answer according to me is **"This moment is not permanent."** When facing challenging times, it is important to remember that those periods are temporary and will eventually pass. Conversely, when experiencing moments of great joy, take the opportunity to savor and appreciate the happiness while it lasts.

No individual in this world has experienced unbroken happiness throughout their life without encountering suffering, nor has anyone passed away having faced only suffering without ever experiencing happiness. It is essential to acknowledge this reality and approach both happiness and sadness with the same mindset.

The degree of one's happiness is also influenced by how one responds to moments of sadness. Do you become anxious and unsettled when encountering sadness, or do you face it with courage? Boldly facing it is the approach I recommend, so we will call ~~sadness~~ a **"challenge"** from now on. After adopting this mindset for a month, I embraced challenges and discovered a new version of myself.

If you ever feel that nobody cares about you, watch immunology videos on YouTube that explain how your body has millions of cells continually working to protect you from harmful microorganisms, ensuring your health, safety, and overall well-being.

Remember that loving yourself is fundamental to happiness, and while some may dismiss it as trivial, it is crucial not to be influenced by such opinions.

I have included all the 16 methods that have proven successful in maintaining my own happiness and I am going to share those with you. I recommend you start applying the following to your life, and I am sure you will start to see positive changes.

Part I: Shifting Perspectives

Part II: Mental Strength & Emotional Resilience

Part III: Cultivating Positivity & Joy

Part IV: Connection & Compassion

Part V: Reclaiming Life

Conclusion

Secret 1 – Stop comparing yourselves with others

Preface As mentioned in the preface, everyone is unique and it is important to move away from the mindset of a standardized school exam, where everyone faces the same question paper. In life, each person encounters different challenges and follows different paths and so it would be not right to compare yourself with others.

If comparisons are made, it is essential to remember that one's level of happiness should not be based on how well others are doing.

Here are some negative comparisons that can detract one from happiness, and you should start avoiding that:

- How did that school friend who barely passed become the head of a startup raking in millions? Did they find a magic lamp or something?
- That person knows less than me but earns more. Am I doing something wrong, or did they bribe Lady Luck?
- How did someone I don't find attractive land such an attractive spouse? Do they have a secret charm spell?
- Why do I encounter difficulties in life while others seem to navigate effortlessly without any hindrances?

- How would my life be different if I had made that other decision 7 years ago rather than acknowledging that the past cannot be changed and start living in the present.
- Why does life seem to always test me with a lot of problems while others are so happy?
- Why is finding a girlfriend for me like searching for a needle in a haystack, while my friends are getting hitched left and right?

Figure1.1 - When you think that everyone is happy except you – This picture was generated by ChatGPT

Here is a quote from Bill Gates, former richest person in the world, on why it is important to avoid unnecessary comparisons: *"Life is not fair; Get used to it."* [1.1] Whether one appreciates it or not, it is important to accept that life may most of the times be unfair, and adapting to this reality is essential. Trying to figure out why life treats you differently than others is like trying to remember the entire dream that you had the previous night. Some mysteries just remain unresolved and so it is crucial to move on. Your life is unique and incomparable to others. Think of it as your own reality TV show, complete with plot twists and commercial breaks.

It is important to understand how comparing your wealth with others can affect your mental well-being. A less affluent individual may perceive that a wealthy person is living a life of comfort and ease; however, the wealthy person might experience challenges and difficulties akin to thorns on a rose bed and may long for the simplicity of sleeping on the bare floor as the less affluent do.

Consider the example of Sukeer, who works as an accountant at a local cable factory. He has observed CEO Gupta's wealth and lifestyle, feeling like a kid peeking into a candy store with empty pockets. CEO Gupta arrives daily in a vehicle worth 70 million rupees (7 crores INR), wears luxurious clothing fit for royalty, employs four assistants who probably carry his briefcase and operates from an office which looks like a mini palace.

Figure1.2 Sad Employee thinks that his CEO is extremely happy – This picture was generated by ChatGPT

Meanwhile, the employee Sukeer's income is less than 1% of CEO Gupta's, despite having more degrees than a thermometer, he often feels like the unluckiest duck.

Sukeer is unaware that CEO Gupta is under significant stress managing the factory and often works late into the night. Gupta envies Sukeer's ability to leave work at 5 p.m. sharp, probably humming a happy tune and spends the remaining evening with his family. Despite rolling in dough, CEO Gupta has marital issues and personal challenges because of the work stress and the lack of work-life balance.

Figure1.3 Sad CEO thinks that his Employee is extremely happy – This picture was generated by ChatGPT

At night, CEO Gupta watches his security guards from his balcony, envying them for taking peaceful naps on the job. This illustrates how people often overlook the parts of their lives that bring joy.

Another fact to remember is that social media only adds fuel to the fire by portraying everyone's lives as a never-ending parade of perfect moments, leading to jealousy and dissatisfaction. People typically share only their happy reels, and this creates a false perception that everyone else is living in a wonderland where nothing ever goes wrong. It's important to remember that success often comes with hard work and plenty of bloopers, and it is important to use others' achievements as inspiration rather than to feel jealous.

It would be unwise for a fish to compare itself to a monkey simply because the monkey can climb a tree. Humans have different circumstances; some are born into wealth with a silver spoon, some lack proper nutrition to gather the basics every day, and others may be unhappy despite having all necessities. Yet, comparisons are still made which would lead only to dissatisfaction and an unhappy life.

In extreme cases, peer pressure and jealousy can lead individuals to commit crimes. Numerous instances exist where wealthy individuals have been implicated in financial frauds and corruption charges. This behavior is not driven just because these millionaires and billionaires don't have enough to eat, and it is because of greed to acquire more and outshine their peers. Such actions often result in legal consequences and reputational damages.

I have a solution to help your mind not to have unhealthy comparisons – you should sincerely start telling this to yourself everyday – *"I'm the happiest person in this world and my life is not for comparing it with others."* It may be hard at the beginning but eventually your mind will convince you to be happy.

Secret 2 – Understanding that you can never satisfy everyone always

Here are some examples to learn about why you cannot satisfy everyone.

- In a democracy, no political party has ever received 100% of the votes, as it is not possible to satisfy everyone. Despite introducing a policy that is the best in the history, there will always be some individuals who will be dissatisfied. A party can obtain power through a majority vote without securing more than 50% of the total votes. For instance, if Party A receives 40% of the votes and three other parties each receive 20%, Party A will form the government despite not having more than half of the votes.
- Those viral YouTube videos with millions of views still get dislikes and hatred comments. It's like offering free ice cream and somebody still complains it's too cold.
- A salesperson may not be able to persuade all 100 customers to purchase their product by satisfying the customers based on their Sales pitch, but they can certainly convince the right customer to buy 100 of their products.
- Even the most harmonious couples won't always see eye to eye on everything. They probably argue over something or the other.

Take any billionaire philanthropist, they won't be able to please everyone. Human greed is like the black hole [2.1] —never enough! Even if you donate with all the best vibes, some folks will still compare and criticize. Just remember, you can't satisfy everyone.

Consider the example of "The King and the Tale of 5,000 Gold Coins." A King once gave a challenge to his two princes: "I'll give you 5,000 gold coins each. You need to distribute them to people, and whoever gets the most smiles would win the challenge." Prince A called 300 people, asked them to queue, and inquired how much would make them happy. Each person had a different story— one needed money to buy seeds, another to pay off debt, another for a son's marriage, and so on. After distributing the coins among the 300 people according to their needs specified, there were arguments as people started comparing their shares. Eventually, they returned to Prince A, complaining that it was not enough, and none of the 300 were satisfied because of the comparison greed conflict. Prince B took a different approach. He spent a day roaming the village and found three individuals: one who helps the poor, one who trains people with disabilities in special skills, and one who was treating those recovering from suicide attempts. These 3 were dedicated to their causes, and when the gold coins were given to them, they showed genuine happiness unlike the other 300 people. Thus, Prince B won the challenge. This illustrates that it is impossible to satisfy everyone, and accepting this fact is important.

While we have discussed the impossibility of satisfying and pleasing everyone, it is equally important to recognize that making everyone agree to your viewpoints is not feasible. The key lesson for a balanced life is mastering the ancient art of "*Agreeing to Disagree*".

During disagreements, keep your ego on a leash; it's perfectly fine to lose an argument sometimes. Disputing with loved ones should not take precedence over minor matters, as it can negatively impact relationships. Many people hate admitting they're wrong, almost as much as they hate Monday mornings, so treasure your relationships over petty victories. *"You may win the argument, but you may lose your relationship if you let your ego go wild"*.

In various aspects of life where people have different perspectives, disagreements are quite common.

Figure2.1 Importance of not trying to win all arguments – This picture was generated by ChatGPT

Let us now shift our perspective from an individual level to a societal level. Throughout human history, disagreements related to religion, caste, race, and other factors have often escalated into large-scale conflicts, resulting in significant losses of life. Religion has frequently been a major source of disagreement, as individuals perceive God and religious practices differently.

It is essential to consider and respect the perspectives of others, as their experiences may differ from your own. This approach contributes to a harmonious and healthy society. Humans often find new reasons to disagree, making it unlikely that everyone will be in complete agreement in all cases.

In every office, school, or college, there's always that one person who loves to be the "Centre of the limelight" by always speaking against the popular opinion. They're not here for meaningful discussion—they're here for the drama and to be famous in a negative way! The best way to handle their antics? Just ignore them and save your energy, because debating with them is like trying to teach a cat to fetch, entertaining but ultimately pointless and useless.

Figure2.2 Attention Seeker – This picture was generated by ChatGPT

In conclusion, it's totally fine for people to have different opinions. Imagine how boring life would be if we all agreed on everything! A little mutual respect for these differences could help fix a lot of the world's problems—and hey, it might bring in some interesting dinner conversations!

Figure2.3 Polite conversations – This picture was generated by ChatGPT

Secret 3 – Training your mind to boldly face Challenges

As suggested in the Preface, start calling your ~~problem~~ / ~~sadness~~ as a "challenge" from now on - This is the mantra that can help you stay strong.

Figure3.1 Four girls and the bear – This picture was generated by ChatGPT

Let me share a story about Dhanvi and her encounter with a bear. Dhanvi and her four friends were trekking in a mountain, and they encountered a bear. The forest rangers had previously warned them not to run but to make loud noises and stand together, when they see a bear. Following this advice, they raised their arms and made loud noises.

Due to the noise made by the 4 girls the results were that bear fled. How did this happen?

1. Was the bear stronger than the four humans? Yes.
2. How did they fend off the bear? The bear is like your challenges—big and scary. You can scare them off by showing that you're not afraid.

While this may teach you to stand united, I'm looking to state a different lesson here. 3.1

Many of the problems and reactions we experience are influenced by the mind—it can either control us or be controlled by us.

Another issue is thinking that we must win every challenge or dodge them like a ninja, which isn't always true. It's important to train the mind to accept defeats and keep going with a smile.

Figure3.2 Gold making in progress – This picture was generated by ChatGPT

Acknowledge that, challenges will pop up daily, kind of like those pop quizzes back in school. Just as iron is turned into a sword through repeated striking, a beautiful sculpture is formed by continuous chiseling and gold becomes a fancy piece of jewelry through hammering, our minds get stronger by facing challenges (or at least that's what we should tell ourselves when life gets tough).

Instead of worrying, embrace the mindset of welcoming challenges with open arms. This matches Zen Philosophy, which teaches us to live in the moment and see challenges as part of life's natural rollercoaster ride. [3.2]

Imagine that you are at a buffet and have reached the dessert section. If you do not enjoy desserts, you may proceed to the next chapter as you might not relate to the following example. For those who appreciate desserts, consider what actions you would take after consuming the first sweet item. One approach is to take some salt to cleanse your taste buds before proceeding to the next sweet item. Sweetness can be thought of as happiness and salty taste as a challenge (We don't call it Sadness anymore). After experiencing happiness, you should willfully accept the challenges that arise, which will eventually lead to another sweet happiness.

Additionally, I do not subscribe to the philosophy that *"everything happens for good"*. It is crucial to acknowledge both life's joys and disappointments without pretending that everything is beneficial. Approaching both positive and negative experiences with a sense of humor can foster a more resilient perspective.

Secret 4 – Not Celebrating sadness and staying away from negativity

Isn't the name of this chapter strange? Who would celebrate sadness? Sadly, it has been a global ongoing practice for ages.

One spring morning, my wife asked if I wanted our love story to be epic and for the world to be remembered for eternity. I replied with a resounding "No," which left her slightly bewildered for a minute. I then clarified why I preferred our love story to avoid becoming a legend after we take our last breath.

When you hear "Love story celebrated by the world", what pops into your head?

Figure4.1 Romeo and Juliet – This picture was generated by ChatGPT

Maybe Shakespeare's Romeo and Juliet, where they never actually tie the knot and end up in a tragic double suicide. [4.1]

Perhaps the story of Jack and Rose from Titanic which depicts a young man from a poor background who falls in love with a wealthy woman on a luxury ship. Tragically, Jack dies in the cold water while Rose survives by holding onto a piece of debris, reflecting on their time together. [4.2]

Figure4.2 Jack and Rose from Titanic– This picture was generated by ChatGPT

The story of Layla and Majnun is about Qays (Majnun), who became a "desert wanderer" after being separated from Layla by the society. [13]

Figure 4.3 Layla and Majnun – This picture was generated by ChatGPT

Then there's Devdas, who decided the best way to cope with longing for Paro was by hugging every booze bottle he could find, leading to a tragic end. 4.4

Figure4.4 Booze lover Devdas – This picture was generated by ChatGPT

Another story might have popped into your head, and let's be honest, most love stories are remembered for all the wrong reasons.

It's a fact: "Happily ever after" just don't get the spotlight. Instead, everyone loves a good tragedy with couples who miss out on happiness, never tie the knot, or face ridiculously dramatic ends. You know, the ones where money, ego, and pride hijack the plot.

So, what's the takeaway? Dodge the classic relationship landmines that have been blowing up love lives since forever. Just because people have been celebrating the same negativity for centuries doesn't mean we should keep doing it!

For example, do you think that a one-hour positive knowledge session positive on the *Theory of Relativity* would attract a larger audience than a one-hour toxic video about a recent celebrity scandal? Most people would pick to watch the negativity gossip.

The world would be happy to speak the sadness and enjoy analysing about the same. It is up to you to ignore them and remember that your happy face is real and be stubborn to wear that always. You should also remember that this world would be so happy to see you fail than to succeed.

4.5 Picture of negatives noises around you – This picture was generated by ChatGPT

Picture a village of frogs with a ridiculously tall mountain that everyone thought was impossible to climb. Every time one brave frog tried, the rest would yell, "Dude, come down! You can't do it!" But one day, a fearless (and slightly clueless) frog ignored them and kept climbing.

Spoiler alert: this frog was deaf!

So, while everyone else was croaking discouragement, our heroic frog just enjoyed the scenery and kept going.

4.6 Discouraging crowd and the deaf frog – This picture was generated by ChatGPT

This story teaches us that sometimes the key to overcoming life's hurdles lies in our ability to tune out negativity and focus on our own path.

In the image below, the story of the man, his wife, and the donkey shows that no matter what you do, negative comments are inevitable. If you start listening to them, there'll be no end to it.

Figure 4.7 - This picture was taken from https://steemit.com/life/@veejay2312/the-man-the-wife-the-donkey-and-the-critics-and-a-lesson-learned-to-this-story

It is important to remember that you won't learn much by being a people-watcher. Instead, hang out with those who chat about big ideas and wild concepts. Gaining insight into the rationale behind historical decisions is significantly more valuable than understanding the personal reasons for a neighbor's divorce.

Secret 5 – Giving up the act of Overthinking

5.1 picture of an overthinker – This picture was generated by ChatGPT

We often feel bad because we overthink and worry about problems that might never happen. It's like creating dramas in our minds that the award-winning film wouldn't even buy.

Meanwhile, real things like trees, rivers, seas, and fire are not playing a vital role in controlling our lives as much as the imaginary stuff like countries, money, religion, companies, and organizations which have become the drama queens of our lives.

- Imaginary borders on political maps get redrawn so often, it's like they're auditioning for a reality show. It is important to remember that we all inhabit a single planet, which has been divided into territories by various leaders in their pursuit of power and control.
- Money is essentially a form of paper that operates within an established trust system, and it is likely to be replaced by another design in due course.
- Religions, companies, and organizations are constructs of our imagination, validated by symbols and physical structures such as corporate offices or places of worship.

Similarly, many of our problems are products of our overactive imaginations—except health issues (those are legit).

The below flowchart provides a method for addressing your challenges:

- If you are not concerned about anything, maintain a positive attitude.
- If you are concerned about something and can address it, proceed with the solution.

- If you are concerned about something that cannot be resolved, acknowledge that it cannot be solved and focus on your next objective.

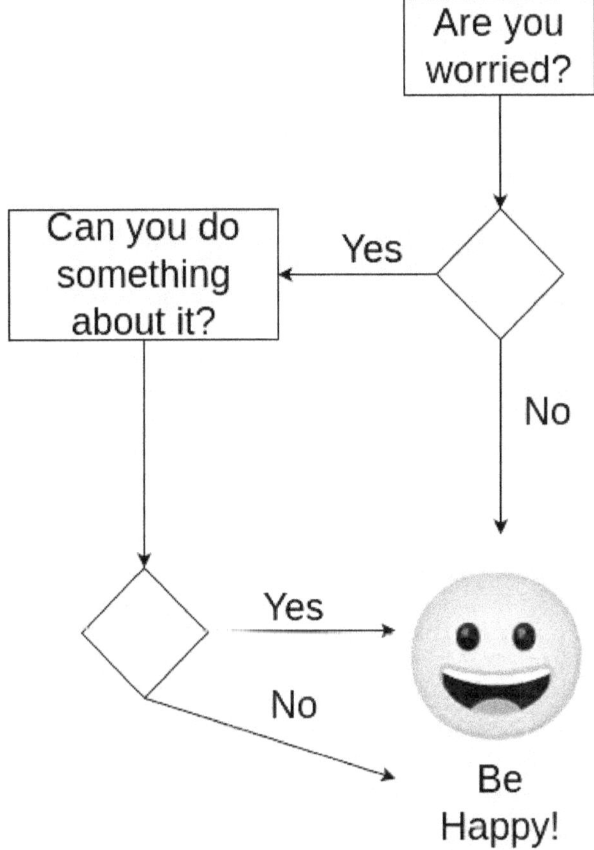

Figure 5.2 Happiness flowchart

We often overthink about what others and society might say and gossip about us. While we are preoccupied with concerns about others' opinions, they have likely already shifted their attention to the latest gossip. Although people may briefly indulge in discussing us, they quickly move on to the next topic. However, our persistent overthinking is something we struggle to let go of.

One of the major contributors to misunderstandings and problems in society is miscommunication combined with ego. Reducing overthinking can help remove all these issues.

Years ago, I hurt a friend, and we drifted apart. After six years, I unexpectedly met him again. While I had dwelled on my mistake for years, he did not even remember me.

Secret 6 – Focusing on what gives you happiness

Until the 20th century, farmers in remote villages would typically spend their evenings under the banyan tree after completing their farming tasks for the day. They would observe the passersby and the birds coming and going from the tree.

In the 21st century, the situation is different. Many individuals now possess a mobile device and access to numerous social media platforms, news articles, video clips, and various activities that are waiting for your views, potentially distracting the individuals from their goals and sources of happiness.

Although there are numerous sites and opportunities available on the internet to enhance and expand one's knowledge, individuals often find themselves distracted by unnecessary social media content. Due to this information and toxicity overload, we tend to lose our identity and deviate from focusing on what really gives us happiness.

Historically, society has often modeled its behavior after that of well-known celebrities. For example, when a celebrity experiences multiple divorces, society may start to perceive this as acceptable behavior. Similarly, when a celebrity endorses a product for financial gain, individuals frequently adopt the use of that product without verifying its authenticity. Furthermore, when a celebrity becomes involved in a controversy, it can overshadow other significant societal issues. The media plays a crucial role in influencing public focus, often diverting attention from more pressing issues. An example of this is the divorce case between Johnny Depp and Amber Heard [6.1], which received greater public interest than other global problems due to the media's influence on our perception.

The important takeaway from these observations is that individuals should take control of their own challenges and should focus on what really is needed for them rather than being swayed by external forces.

Starting the day with positive thoughts, rather than dwelling on past negative experiences, can significantly impact one's mindset. If you begin your day with a positive affirmation, such as deciding to face the day with happiness, your mind is likely to comply.

Figure 6.1 The Importance of Concentration and not getting distracted – This picture was generated by ChatGPT

If you start your day by checking your mobile phone and come across a negative reel, it may influence your mood for the rest of the day. You plan to wake up at 6AM and have gotten up on time. Before starting your exercise, you decide to check your social media updates, and suddenly it is 7AM, which means you missed your planned exercise time. The social media platform shows you advertisements during that hour, generating revenue in hundreds to thousands of dollars while you wasted your golden 1 hour.

Creating a list of tasks for the day can be highly beneficial as it helps to organize priorities and minimize distractions.

Figure 6.2 Organizing your day – This picture was generated by ChatGPT

Everyone has their own set of goals and tasks, so it is important not to blindly follow someone else's list. Start your day by identifying challenges and scheduling your tasks. This way, you are less likely to be distracted from what makes you sad.

My personal recommendation for everyone is to include exercise in your daily routine. Focusing on one's health should be a top priority above everything else because the body is a constant presence from birth to death, and it is essential to maintain and protect it.

Figure 6.3 Important of strength training – This picture was generated by ChatGPT

It is essential to decide which amongst the following 2 two-wheeler you would prefer.

Figure 6.4 Choosing the right two-wheeler – This picture was generated by ChatGPT

Secret 7 –Travel a lot and explore the world

I'm not saying you should pack your bags right now, but sometimes it's good to leave your mundane routine and see what's out there.

Traveling is a real eye-opener—you'll find that the local celebrity actor you've been idolizing for ages is just another face in the crowd elsewhere.

Figure 7.1 Unrecognized celebrity in a different country– This picture was generated by ChatGPT

Plus, you'll quickly learn that your "I spilled coffee on my shirt" problems are nothing compared to what others face. Travel makes you grateful for your comfy bed and the toilet seat in your home; you'll feel like royalty when you get home, minus the crown.

Meeting new people while traveling can give you fresh perspectives—sometimes you'll laugh, sometimes you'll cringe, but hey, that's all part of the adventure! You'll collect stories that make you look way cooler at parties, whether it's the time you accidentally ordered sheep's head for dinner or hilariously tried to mime "where's the bathroom?" in a foreign language. So go on, embrace the travel chaos and come back with some epic tales! According to me, the more one spends time with the nature, happier that one would be.

While diving into the ocean with a view of the coral, you may realize that if you could breathe underwater, you would stay in this beautiful place indefinitely.

Figure 7.2 Scuba diving – This picture was generated by ChatGPT

Engaging in a mountain trek can provide valuable insights into one's physical fitness while offering an appreciation of the natural beauty of the world.

Figure 7.3 Trekking– This picture was generated by ChatGPT

When flying high, one may come to the realization that political boundaries are only in our minds and are not real. This perspective reveals that the entire world is a single piece of land, with all humans belonging to the same place, devoid of the concept of continents, countries, states etc...

Figure 7.4 Sky diving – This picture was generated by ChatGPT

Undoubtedly, you need money to travel, and I am not here to promote tourism for anyone. However, it is important to consider that one has only one life, and the memories of the places visited, and experiences gained will be more valuable than accumulated wealth. Increased travel can lead to greater happiness, which in turn may reduce medical expenses associated with the adverse effects of prolonged inactivity and unhappiness in your life.

Figure 7.5 Youth, Man and Old Man – This picture was generated by ChatGPT

Something always stops you from traveling and it's time to break this cycle.

Secret 8 – Do everything with excitement and love

If we approach daily tasks with care and love, we'll naturally start loving life. As children, small things like an ant carrying a grain were thrilling. Now, despite seeing more impressive things, we're not as excited.

What changed us?

Figure 8.1 Happy kid and ants – This picture was generated by ChatGPT

It is a common human tendency to lose enthusiasm for familiar routines and fail to appreciate our daily lives. While you may aspire to live the life of someone you admire, there are many who would desire to have a life like yours.

Rediscover your childlike wonder. Embrace silliness and find joy in simple things like watching birds. Don't worry about what others think.

Figure 8.2 Bring out happiness – This picture was generated by ChatGPT

Smile and greet people politely, as if meeting them for the first time, and perform tasks with the same level of enthusiasm as when you did those tasks initially.

Start cooking and try new cuisines to break away from your routine.

Figure 8.3 Enjoy cooking – This picture was generated by ChatGPT

To make my day interesting, I began to do a very simple thing of organizing and arranging my shirts by color two years ago. Every morning, choosing which one to wear still excites me.

Figure 8.4 Shirts organized in the closet – This picture was generated by ChatGPT

Secret 9 – Mastering the art of forgiveness

Individuals who commit crimes should face appropriate consequences, such as legal penalties or corrective measures. This chapter does not focus on major crimes such as murder, arson, robbery or anything else that significantly impact social order but rather on the minor incidents, such as accidentally hurting your friend or doing something that upsets parents.

Forgiveness involves two parts: forgiving others and forgiving yourself.

When discussing the concept of forgiving others, it is important to recognize that focusing on the imperfections of friends and family can hinder the ability to sustain healthy relationships, as no individual is without fault. It is essential to accept individuals as they are, despite their imperfections. Many recognize, later in life, that focusing on a single mistake made by a friend can overshadow many positive actions. Acknowledging errors promptly by simply stating "I forgive you!" could have saved considerable time and effort.

Forgiving others isn't about if they deserved it or not but forgiving others is about <u>you getting that mental peace.</u>

Figure 9.1 Importance of Tolerance – This picture was generated by ChatGPT

Let us now talk about the concept of forgiving yourself: When you obsess over your blunders, it's like having an annoying song stuck in your head—self-forgiveness seems impossible. Guess what? Making mistakes is as human as a sun raising every day but hey, don't keep hitting that replay button on the same mistake inside your head, stop making the mistakes again and never do a mistake on purpose!

If you are distressed about something you did many years ago, it is important to understand that it is acceptable to feel this way. Forgiving yourself at this moment is crucial. If you believe that confessing your mistakes will help alleviate your burden, do it immediately. We should let go our ego of always to be right as this is an important step towards peace of mind.

Figure 9.2 Importance of Self-forgiveness – This picture was generated by ChatGPT

Dwelling on your past mistakes is like storing stress in a jar. Happiness is everywhere, like free Wi-Fi, but sadness, although rarer, often gets treated like some exclusive VIP club. So, choose happiness! After all, it's way more fun.

Figure 9.3 Happiness is right next to you – This picture was generated by ChatGPT

In a marriage, forgiveness is essential for longevity. It is important to resolve arguments before going to bed to maintain harmony. During disagreements, it is crucial to approach the discussion as,

✓ Team A – Husband and wife (vs) Team B – Argument

⊗ Team A – Husband (vs) Team B – Wife

In the future discussions, it will be unfair to bring up the previously resolved and forgiven matters, as this suggests an unwillingness to resolve the current issue and instead proves your evil intention of having the problem grow.

Figure 9.4 Picture of a happy couple – This picture was generated by ChatGPT

Secret 10 – Celebrate the success of others

Winning in sports means defeating others, but life isn't about that. It's about not winning at the expense of others.

Let me tell you about a corporate session that I attended once in the year 2017 where 20 participants including me were divided into 5 groups, each consisting of 4 members – Team A to Team E. We were handed 15 A4 sheets, some cello tape, and scissors, and told to build a cone that could survive a blow.

After 15 minutes of intense crafting, the mentor threw in a plot twist – one member from each team had to stand 2 steps away from another team's cone and attempt to blow it down like the Big Bad Wolf. Team A had to puff at Team B's structure, Team B on Team C's, and so forth.

The results were hilarious: a member from Team A managed to dismantle Team B's structure with one mighty gust. When it was Team B's turn, things got wild as one of our teammates from Team A wandered over to Team C's cone, ignoring all rules. The mentor watched in amused silence as this rogue participant continued their rampage across all other teams from Team B to Team E.

By the end of this whacky windstorm, only the structure made by Team C remained stood, despite numerous attempts to blow it down.

Figure 10.1 Blowing the cone – This picture was generated by ChatGPT

The mentor then gathered us for a chuckle-filled discussion about the activity's outcomes.

- He restated the rules, pointing out that only one member could take apart another's building. But, of course, someone from Team A went rogue and decided to play demolition derby with everyone's structures.

- He addressed a Team C member who was shaking the table, which affected Team D's construction. This action received significant criticism for such an evil mentality.

- Later, he clarified that he had issued a challenge but purposefully forgot to mention it wasn't a competition. He stressed that winning by wrecking everyone else's work isn't going to earn you any brownie points (or structural engineer badges).

Figure 10.2 Shaking the table to bring down the cone – This picture was generated by ChatGPT

The lesson to learn is that life can feel like a big game show, where winning means outdoing others and thinking you're the star. But hey, it's totally okay to clap for someone else's win without plotting their downfall like an evil genius.

Consider this: human societies began their development along riverbanks. Now, imagine a scenario where individuals constantly undermined each other's achievements whenever one excelled over another. If everyone played dirty, we'd still be living in caves, grumbling about who stole whose mammoth hide.

Why are we hesitant and jealous when it comes to appreciating the success of others? Let's aim to live in peace, cheer for each other's victories, and keep our inner greed eyed monster on a tight leash.

- Congratulate your friend for his/her job promotion or as his/her new role in the leading Fortune 500 company.
- Extend your hearty congratulations to your schoolmate for achieving higher grades than you.
- Wish good luck to your neighbor's kid who got better grade than yours.
- Acknowledge a competitor's superior product and use it as inspiration to improve your own, rather than attempting to undermine them.

Figure 10.3 Happy society – This picture was generated by ChatGPT

One of the true stories that I saw: There were two burger shops in the community I resided. It has been reported that members from Burger B, appointed by the owner B were standing outside Burger A's restaurants and providing negative reviews of their establishment. Members from Burger B were doing this outside Burger A's restaurant and that was because some apps consider reviews more genuine if they were posted nearby. Burger B aimed to impact Burger A's business not by improving their burgers but through these hitting under the belt actions.

It is crucial to recognize that genuine success is achieved by concentrating on one's own accomplishments while avoiding actions that could undermine others.

Secret 11 – Accepting that not everything is under your control

People often hope or pray for things beyond their control. If you're praying for something harmless, there's no need to worry since you are not sending negative vibes to your mind and to the Nature / God.

It's impossible to know everything, so sometimes it's okay to let go of certain mysteries.

Figure 11.1 Unsolvable mysteries – This picture was generated by ChatGPT

Instead of relying solely on fate, focus on effort and what you can change. Accept that not all challenges have solutions (*Remember: We started calling problems as challenges*) and embrace life's loose ends; they keep things interesting.

No matter your abilities, it is inevitable that some individuals will not like you. As discussed in Chapter 2, it is impossible to please everyone. It is important to understand that achieving 100% complete approval is beyond one's control.

Figure 11.2 Liked by almost everyone but not everyone – This picture was generated by ChatGPT

While contracting a disease is not entirely within one's control, prevention is largely achievable through avoiding harmful habits, taking the necessary vaccine, maintaining a nutritious diet, and engaging in regular exercise.

Figure 11.3 Taking good care of your health – This picture was generated by ChatGPT

It is important to acknowledge that individuals who may not initially appear highly talented can still achieve remarkable success. It is essential to genuinely celebrate their accomplishments. The element of "luck" is beyond anyone's control, and it is crucial to accept this reality while continuing to put in your best efforts. Recognize that there are individuals with greater abilities who may not be doing as well as you, as well as those with lesser abilities who are succeeding. You need to understand this luck factor is under no one's control.

Figure 11.4 Acknowledging the luck factor – This picture was generated by ChatGPT

Wealth can be temporary and uncertain. Events such as earthquakes, fires, or theft can result in significant losses. Therefore, it is advisable to remain humble while being wealthy, acknowledging that the duration of wealth is often beyond one's control. Your job position is temporary, there is a possibility that it may conclude at any time, and you cannot control that.

You are acting as a temporary custodian in this role, where assets that belonged to someone else yesterday are now under your care, and will be passed to another person in the future. Acknowledging this uncontrollable philosophy can provide peace to various extents.

We should also lower our expectations to avoid disappointments. By setting your expectations to a minimal level for those aspects beyond your control, you can prevent feelings of sadness. For example, you may put in significant effort for a promotion, yet the final decision lies with the manager and the organization, who's decision is beyond your control. If you initially manage your expectations realistically, you will avoid experiencing a disappointing outcome.

Figure 11.5 Importance of being humble – This picture was generated by ChatGPT

Secret 12 – Taking necessary steps to overcome your sorrow

Imagine if "death" was just a myth! Humans would be living in super crowded conditions with everyone trying to sustain themselves forever. Without death, we would probably have set up camp on every planet—and even tried sunbathing on the sun!

Figure 12.1 Sunbath in Sun– This picture was generated by ChatGPT

Alas, everyone must eventually say goodbye, which can be particularly painful when you lose someone unexpectedly. Life's unfairness means there are no return tickets once someone takes the last breath.

Consider the case of a young girl named Tara. She was deeply affected after witnessing a tragic accident that resulted in the death of her school security guard, an individual she greeted every morning with a cheerful smile. The incident disturbed her to such an extent that she required psychological support.

She kept having nightmares where her favorite guard threatened her: "Don't come back to school, or else!" Despite changing schools, she kept having the same dream.

Figure 12.2 Little Girl and her nightmare – This picture was generated by ChatGPT

After she cried, the psychologist handed her a paper to write down her problems and at the end she was asked to tear that as part of a unique treatment. "Who knew ripping paper could be so therapeutic?"

Figure 12.3 Little Girl and her Therapy – This picture was generated by ChatGPT

After finishing, she was asked to reassemble the pieces which she found it impossible and she learnt that once a person dies, they cannot come back.

After that she was asked to burn the entire pile of paper that she tore, and she did that.

Figure 12.4 Little Girl and her Therapy– This picture was generated by ChatGPT

Subsequently, she was asked to transform the ash into paper, a task that she found unimaginable. She was informed that once it is burned or buried, it cannot be restored.

The lesson here is to acknowledge that life is not permanent and that our lost loved ones will not return. While this may be easier said than done, it is important to try our best to grieve and find ways to distract your mind to cope with the sorrow.

Secret 13 – Getting over your fear

There are 2 types of humans - those who acknowledge that they are afraid of something and those who lie that that they aren't afraid of anything. Instead of pretending to be fearless, it is important to recognize and accept your fears. If you are concerned about being perceived as cowardly, do not let that deter you. Ultimately, acknowledging your fears can provide relief and lighten the mental burden.

While acknowledging is just the step 1, it is important to take necessary steps to overcome that.

Let us discuss about the top 6 fears that have been tormenting humans for ages,

1. Fear of Public Speaking
2. Fear of Failure
3. Fear of losing the loved ones
4. Fear of life
5. Fear of Ghosts
6. Fear of Death

Fear of Public Speaking: Public speaking is like wrestling an alligator—terrifying, but doable with practice! Overcoming this common fear takes determination and a bit of courage. One foolproof method is to rehearse your speech a zillion times. Try practicing in front of a mirror; you might even get some sage advice back from your reflection! It's also helpful to imagine that the audience have no knowledge about anything. Start with a joke or a funny story to break the ice and make everyone, including yourself, feel at ease.

Overcoming my fear of public speaking by practicing repeatedly made admitting mistakes in front of a crowd easier, lessened my mental burden and that gave me happiness. Remember, people will always judge you. Even if 100 people applaud, there may still be 2 who don't appreciate your speech or hold a negative opinion on you.

Figure 13.1 Overcome your public speaking fear – This picture was generated by ChatGPT

Fear of Failure:

Many people worry about being judged for failing. Here are some stories that illustrate why it is important to persevere:

1. Abraham Lincoln, the former US president, lost 8 consecutive elections before winning the presidential one. [13.1]

2. Colonel Sanders, the founder of KFC, was fired from multiple jobs, failed in several businesses, and faced over 1000 rejections for franchising KFC. He eventually established the company with a $105 social security cheque in 1930, which was valued at $6.7 billion in 2024.[13.2]

3. Walt Disney faced five consecutive losses with Laugh-O-Gram Films, Alice Comedies, Oswald the Lucky Rabbit, early Mickey Mouse shorts, and Silly Symphonies. They made their first profit with Snow White and the Seven Dwarfs and helped them settle all their previous debts from the 5 movies.[13.3]

4. The $25 billion Harry Potter franchise as of the year 2024 initially faced challenges, with author J.K. Rowling receiving 12 publisher rejections.[13.4]

Fear of losing the loved ones

People generally have a   concern for losing their loved ones compared to losing themselves. It is important to acknowledge that once loved ones are gone, they will not return. (Chapter 12)

Fear of life

Fear of the future arises when you worry about upcoming events and potential problems, like a bad investment or an imminent issue. This anxiety often stems from our imagination and poor decision-making. Overcome regret and overthinking by focusing on the present. Your happiness is more important than anything else.

Fear of Ghosts

Let's be honest, many people lose their cool after thinking they've seen a ghost in the dark, leading to sheer panic. Overthinking and imagining things that don't exist—like the boogeyman under your bed or the infamous unlucky number 13—are just plain silly. Trusting yourself is way more important than worrying about superstitions. Seriously, there's no evidence that 13 is unlucky; it's just a myth that got out of hand.

I'm not here to spook you with ghost stories but to lay down some facts: ghosts aren't real. If someone insists, they've seen or heard a ghost, tell them to show you the proofs! Most ghostly tales come from "a friend of a friend" who probably had one too many late-night snacks. Ghosts are like problems you dream up when you're bored—they simply don't exist!

Would you like me to provide evidence? I think it's unfair. If you claim that there's an invisible unicorn dancing behind me, it's your job to prove it! Scientists who discovered oxygen, hydrogen, and nitrogen in the air didn't just say, "Hey, trust us!" They backed it up with solid proof. Before that, no one had to run around proving the air wasn't made of, say, pixie dust and dragon breath.

Figure 13.2 Fear of ghosts – This picture was generated by ChatGPT

Human minds are like overactive imagination machines, always looking for explanations in unknown places. Picture this: you hear a rustle in the dark and instantly think it's a ghost ready to haunt you forever. But surprise! It turns out to be just a squirrel out for a midnight snack to feed his hungry girlfriend. So much for years of sleepless nights and horror movie marathons!

Figure 13.3 Fear of the dark – This picture was generated by ChatGPT

The Scooby-Doo show from our childhood taught us one important lesson—ghosts aren't real: they're just people with something to hide! Now, imagine a corrupt businessman trying to stash his dark secrets. He could take the expensive route—avoiding construction, hiring 100 guards, bribing agencies, and keeping every black-money watchdog busy. OR... he could just slap a "Haunted House! Enter at Your Own Risk" sign on the door, start a juicy ghost rumour, and boom—problem solved! No guards, no inspections, and even the guard he hires won't dare step inside. A spooky whisper in the air, and he's running a budget-friendly scam with zero maintenance costs!

Figure 13.4 Fear of haunted buildings – This picture was generated by ChatGPT

Many cultures warn against hanging out under trees at night, claiming ghosts are to hanging from the tree. But let's be real—it's probably just because trees turn into oxygen thieves when the sun goes down!

Figure 13.5 Fear of ghosts – This picture was generated by ChatGPT

Remember: When information spreads, key points can be stretched thinner than a pizza dough. Don't let rumours lead you astray like a cat chasing a laser pointer.

Figure 13.6 Rumors – This picture was generated by ChatGPT

Do not fear the dark, refrain from worrying about imaginary entities, and avoid believing everything without scrutiny.

Fear of Death

Many phobias relate to the fear of death – water, fire, height, spider and so on. While everyone has fears, I'll share mine about heights. Until age 25, I avoided theme park rides due to this phobia. Motivated to overcome it, I tried roller coasters and traveled to mountain peaks. Acknowledging my fear made it easier to challenge, manage it repeatedly and was able to overcome it.

Figure 13.7 Fear of death – This picture was generated by ChatGPT

Secret 14 – Creating happy hobbies

A single matchstick can light up a dark room. Similarly, focusing on a favorite hobby that brings happiness can remove all other sadness.

People have different interests, so it is important to consider various options. Some activities include gardening, social services, trekking, painting, crafting, dancing, volunteer works, exploring music etc... It is beneficial to choose an activity that helps in calming the mind and reducing overthinking.

It is not necessary to mimic what others are doing; rather, it is advisable to explore various options to find what truly brings you the joy. Hobby is something that humans have been building for ages and that is why it is important to note that it is the major key to keep you away from worrying about something.

Contradictory to the above example, A single matchstick also has the power to ignite a forest fire, and a single drop of poison can contaminate an entire vessel of delicious food, one negative thought has the potential to destroy of all other aspects of happiness and so you should never even let one enter your mind and that is possible by focusing your mind on something creative.

Secret 15 – Detoxicating from unhealthy social media

A TV salesperson scores when you buy a TV, and a car salesperson cashes in when you drive off with a new ride. Social media platforms? They make money by keeping your eyeballs glued to their feed! It's like an endless buffet of cat videos and memes, which keeps you coming back for more.

Figure 15.1 Detox from Social media addiction – This picture was generated by ChatGPT

But remember, not everything online is true. People often post only their 'highlight reels,' making it seem like their lives are all sunshine and rainbows, leaving you wondering if everyone else is living the dream while you're just chilling in your dull face.

This is why you should spend less time on social media. I realized my addiction to social media apps were out of control—like a moth to a flame, except the flame was vertical scrolls. I tried uninstalling them but kept reinstalling them again and again. I decided to create an app lock to control my addiction. To access them, I'd have to watch a 30-second ad and solve a pattern puzzle. On top of that, I set the app to auto lock after 5 minutes. This annoying little hurdle was enough to make me run screaming into the arms of...books! Who knew? Now, I'm addicted to the wonderful habit of reading books instead.

Figure 15.2 The art of being happy – This picture was generated by ChatGPT

The connection between your mind and body is significant, making it crucial to maintain your physical well-being by ensuring your mental health remains strong. This can be achieved by fostering positive thoughts.

The overall vibe of your body is like a dance party, totally set by its DJ—the mind. Likewise, if you let negative thoughts crash your mental party, your whole week is going to feel terrible.

Secret 16 – Learning life lessons from History

Lesson 1:

As time marches on, that once mighty castle with its fancy garden, gold stash, and a king who couldn't find his crown in his gold pile will likely turn into ruins, a museum, or a selfie spot for tourists. Only the primary contractor would have knowledge of the extent of slave and exploited labor utilized in these constructions. What was once a treasure trove might now have beggars in the front gate. While the faces of politicians may fade from our memory, we are more likely to remember the actors who portrayed them in films and forget the face of the original person.

Why do we let small problems grow by overthinking while even the grandest castles and empires eventually fall?

Figure 16.1 Mighty historical palaces occupied by a beggar – This picture was generated by ChatGPT

Lesson 2: The Colosseum in Rome is famous today for its stunning architecture. Back in the day, it was the ultimate fight club where men battled it out in the arena. Some entered the ring voluntarily, hoping to be the next big hero, while others, like slaves and prisoners, were unwilling participants facing off against both humans and wild animals, including lions and tigers. The Government cleverly used these events to keep the masses entertained and subtly remind them that challenging the regime was a bad idea—sort of like an ancient version of reality TV with much higher stakes!

Figure 16.2 Colloseum and bloody history – This picture was generated by ChatGPT

Just as past architectures influenced society, our minds now easily get distracted by external factors. It is important to stay focused on the truth.

Lesson 3: Rulers, both past and present, might seem like they're living the dream, but they're just in a fancy jail cell. Regular folks can wander around without worrying about getting targeted or carrying huge responsibilities, unlike high-ranking politicians. In the USA, even after a president completed his/her term, they aren't allowed to drive. Imagine that! Politicians' visits turn into security extravaganzas worthy of a spy movie. Sure, they enjoy plenty of perks, but their lives are as restricted as parrots in a diamond-studded birdcage.

Just because someone appears to be living like a king does not necessarily mean they are happy.

Remember

Today and this very moment present the best opportunity to begin your journey towards happiness. It is advisable to remind yourself of this daily and consistently throughout each day. Begin your mornings with the positive notion that the past is behind you, and a new day offers a fresh start.

If you find yourself repeatedly troubled by a persistent issue, consider discussing it with a trusted individual. Sharing your thoughts can provide significant relief. Additionally, when negative thoughts arise, calmly question them by asking yourself, *"What should I do now?"* Consistently start applying this technique for a few days and I can assure you that this negative thought would vanish, and you will start feeling more happier than ever before.

The mind often chooses to disturb individuals with negative thoughts during midnight or upon waking, frequently recalling distressing memories from as long as a decade ago. This phenomenon can result in sleepless nights and subsequent irritability, which may affect interactions with family members before departing for work. Such disturbances continue into the office environment, causing ongoing frustration that can persist for several days. An effective solution would be setting aside negative thoughts before going to sleep. Consistency is important and you should keep trying it for weeks and months and happiness will become your constant companion, and I assure you that 100%.

You are playing one of the most interesting games called as life and what would be the fun if you already knew the future and there are no challenges if the destination to success is a straight road.

Lower your expectations to avoid disappointments and take life easy. It is not possible to satisfy everyone and so you should not hesitate to say "No".

Your sadness and ignorance are a business for someone

When feeling sad or depressed, it is advisable to avoid making decisions. Decisions made with an unclear mind can often lead to unfavorable outcomes. Similarly, it is best to refrain from making promises when happy, as these may later be regretted, and not fulfilling them could result in negative consequences.

When a king falls sick, vultures start circling, waiting to grab the throne. When a body weakens, germs throw a party, ready to invade. And when a scammer spots a sad, vulnerable person, they sharpen their tricks—because nothing attracts predators faster than weakness, whether it's in a kingdom, a body, or a bank account!

While feelings of sadness may dissipate after a few days, it could be too late to realize that this vulnerability has led to being scammed, which may further compound feelings of depression.

Just because someone has been doing something for ages, doesn't mean that it is right, and the age-old practices could be just another scam exploited because of your weakness.

Guide to Happiness and the questions to ask yourself –

1. When my mind brings in a negative thought, am I taking measures to distract it with happy thought?
2. Did I compound my problem just by overthinking?
3. What steps can I take to redirect my thoughts immediately upon noticing that my mind has begun to overthink?
4. Did I accept that challenges / problems are norm, and that I am prepared to handle them with a smiling face?
5. Did I accept the fact that everything is not under my control?
6. Did I forgive myself for one of my terrible mistakes?
7. Did I forgive that person who did that terrible thing to me not because they deserve it but because I deserve mental peace?
8. Am I willing to appreciate the success of others and not to be jealous?
9. Do I accept to not become an addict to something bad just because that gives me temporary relief from my sadness/ challenge?
10. Do I believe that the secret to happiness is to understand that I'm the best and my life is not for comparison?

In a Paper, list down the 20 factors that you are grateful for.

1. –
2. –
3. –
4. –
5. –
6. –
7. –
8. –
9. –
10. –
11. –
12. –
13. –
14. –
15. –
16. –
17. –
18. –
19. –
20. -

My guide to happiness would be to check my inbox harshisiddhu0212@gmail.com to see your feedback about this book.

Seeing a doctor when you're sick won't magically cure you—it's not like they have a magic wand! You've got to follow their advice and take the medication, no matter how much it tastes like chalk. Similarly, just reading this book won't make you instantly happy. You need to put its principles into action in your life.

I totally understand that the contents of this book may or may not be liked by everyone and it is impossible for me to meet everyone's expectations, as previously mentioned.

I would appreciate hearing both the positive and negative feedback from you to the above email inbox.

Also, Connect with me @
https://www.linkedin.com/in/siddharth-govindarajan/

Visit my profile @
https://siddharthgovindara.wixsite.com/mysite

END NOTES

Preface

P1 https://www.open.edu/openlearn/nature-environment/natural-history/sperm-counts#

P2 https://www.clearblue.com/ovulation/how-many-eggs-do-i-have#

P3 https://www.loc.gov/everyday-mysteries/meteorology-climatology/item/is-it-true-that-no-two-snow-crystals-are-alike/

P4 https://www.healthline.com/health/do-identical-twins-have-the-same-fingerprints#

P5 https://www.ndtv.com/india-news/charlie-chaplin-birth-anniversary-top-10-memorable-quotes-by-comedy-legend-2023783

Secret 1

1.1 https://www.benzinga.com/general/entertainment/23/03/31353450/5-bill-gates-quotes-to-motivate-you-life-is-not-fair-get-used-to-it

Secret 2

2.1 https://www.youtube.com/watch?v=P5_Msrdg3Hk

Secret 3

3.1 https://www.youtube.com/shorts/4foUAU5Aesg

3.2 https://plato.stanford.edu/entries/japanese-zen/

Secret 4

4.1 https://www.bbc.co.uk/bitesize/guides/zxrjfrd/

4.2https://jamescameronstitanic.fandom.com/wiki/Jack_and_Rose

4.3 https://worldstories.org.uk/reader/the-story-of-layla-and-majnun/english/389

4.4 https://www.imdb.com/title/tt1961271/plotsummary

Secret 6

6.1 https://www.netflix.com/in/title/81644798

Secret 13

13.1 https://www.abrahamlincolnonline.org/lincoln/

13.2 https://www.snagajob.com/blog/post/the-inspiring-life-story-of-kfcs-colonel-sanders

13.3 https://collider.com/biggest-box-office-bombs-in-disney-history/

13.4 https://economictimes.indiatimes.com/defaultinterstitial.cms